ETHIOPIA

...in Pictures

Visual Geography Series®

ETHIOPIA

...in Pictures

Prepared by
Daniel Abebe

Lerner Publications Company
Minneapolis

Independent Picture Service

An Ethiopian musician plays a stringed instrument called a *kerar*.

This book is an all-new edition in the Visual Geography Series. Previous editions were published by Sterling Publishing Company, New York City. The text, set in 10/12 Century Textbook, is fully revised and updated, and new photographs, maps, charts, and captions have been added.

Website address: www.lernerbooks.com

LIBRARY OF CONGRESS CATALOGING-IN-PUBLICATION DATA

Abebe, Daniel
  Ethiopia in pictures / prepared by Daniel Abebe.
    p. cm. — (Visual geography series)
  Rev. ed. of: Ethiopia in pictures / Alfred Allotey Acquaye. [1973].
  Includes index.
  Summary: Brief text and photographs introduce the geography, history, government, people, and economy of Ethiopia.
  ISBN 0–8225–1836–8 (lib. bdg.)
  1. Ethiopia. [1. Ethiopia] I. Acquaye, Alfred Allotey. Ethiopia in pictures. II. Title. III. Series: Visual geography series (Minneapolis, Minn.)
DT373.A575 1988
963—dc19   87–27034

International Standard Book Number: 0–8225–1836–8
Library of Congress Catalog Card Number: 87–27034

VISUAL GEOGRAPHY SERIES®

Publisher
Harry Jonas Lerner
Associate Publisher
Nancy M. Campbell
Senior Editor
Mary M. Rodgers
Editor
Gretchen Bratvold
Illustrations Editor
Karen A. Sirvaitis
Consultants/Contributors
Daniel Abebe
Sandra K. Davis
Designer
Jim Simondet
Cartographer
Carol F. Barrett
Indexer
Sylvia Timian
Production Manager
Gary J. Hansen

Independent Picture Service

Irrigated plots help some farmers to produce food for their families.

Acknowledgments

Title page photo courtesy of Tony Fennerty, M.D., and Bogdan Szajkowski, Ph.D.

Elevation contours adapted from *The Times Atlas of the World,* seventh comprehensive edition (New York: Times Books, 1985).

4 5 6 7 8 9 10 – JR – 04 03 02 01 00 99 98

Both modern and traditional methods of transportation are used throughout Ethiopia.

Contents

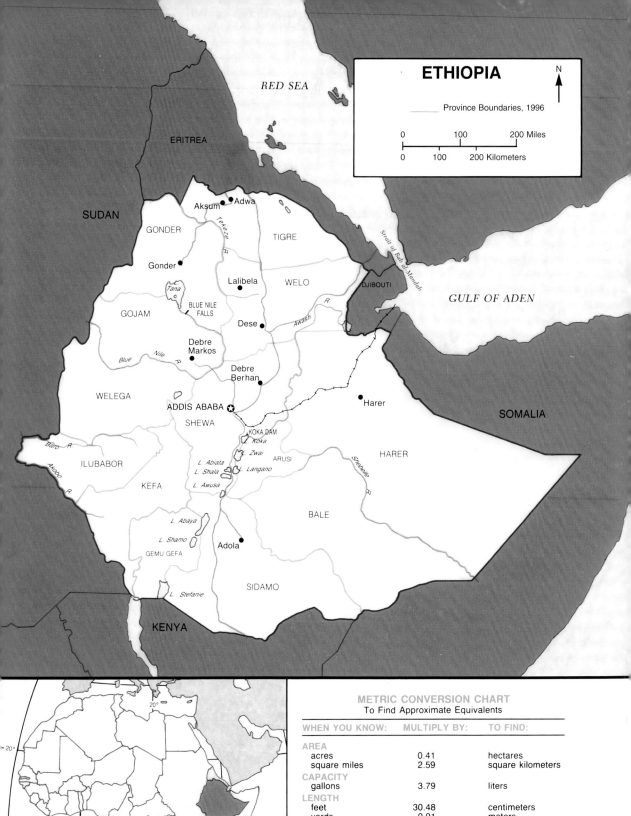

ETHIOPIA

N

Province Boundaries, 1996

| 0 | 100 | 200 Miles |
| 0 | 100 | 200 Kilometers |

RED SEA

ERITREA

SUDAN

GONDER

Aksum • Adwa

TIGRE

Gonder •

Lalibela

WELO

Tana

GOJAM

BLUE NILE
FALLS

Dese

Awash R.

Debre
Markos

Blue *Nile* R.

Debre
Berhan

WELEGA

ADDIS ABABA ✪

SHEWA

Harer •

Baro R.

KOKA DAM
L. Koka

Akobo R.

ILUBABOR

L. Abiata
L. Shala
L. Zwai
Langano

ARUSI

HARER

KEFA

L. Awusa

Shebelle R.

BALE

L. Abaya

L. Shamo

Adola •

SIDAMO

GEMU GEFA

L. Stefanie

KENYA

Tekeze R.

DJIBOUTI

Strait of Bab al-Mandab

GULF OF ADEN

SOMALIA

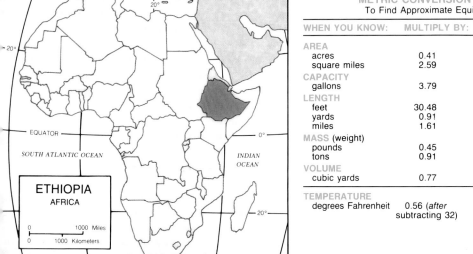

20°

20°

EQUATOR

SOUTH ATLANTIC OCEAN

INDIAN
OCEAN

0°

20°

ETHIOPIA
AFRICA

| 0 | 1000 Miles |
| 0 | 1000 Kilometers |

METRIC CONVERSION CHART
To Find Approximate Equivalents

WHEN YOU KNOW:	MULTIPLY BY:	TO FIND:
AREA		
acres	0.41	hectares
square miles	2.59	square kilometers
CAPACITY		
gallons	3.79	liters
LENGTH		
feet	30.48	centimeters
yards	0.91	meters
miles	1.61	kilometers
MASS (weight)		
pounds	0.45	kilograms
tons	0.91	metric tons
VOLUME		
cubic yards	0.77	cubic meters
TEMPERATURE		
degrees Fahrenheit	0.56 (*after* subtracting 32)	degrees Celsius

Collecting water for household use is usually the job of Ethiopian women. Here, several villagers gather at a well and help one another carry home the filled water containers.

Introduction

Ethiopia, one of Africa's oldest nations, escaped domination by colonial powers for 3,000 years. Its rich history has left a legacy of diverse ethnic groups and many languages. Ethiopia is attempting to emerge as a modern state while preserving its ancient traditions.

Until 1974 Ethiopia was a monarchy ruled by kings, queens, emperors, and empresses. But in that year a military coup d'état put an end to the reign of Haile Selassie. After his downfall, the new government took over businesses and industries and established a strong alliance with the Soviet Union.

The new leader, Mengistu Haile-Mariam, imposed a harsh dictatorship on Ethiopia.

During the 1980s, a civil war raged between government forces and guerrillas fighting for the independence of Eritrea, a northern province. The fighting caused widespread destruction and starvation in the countryside.

In 1991 the war ended with the victory of the Ethiopian People's Revolutionary Democratic Front (EPRDF). Mengistu fled the capital, and a new government under Meles Zenawi took power. This administration could not prevent a formal vote for independence by Eritrea in 1993. Although Ethiopia's economy has partially recovered from years of civil war, Zenawi must still convince rival ethnic groups to cooperate in rebuilding the nation.

7

Called Tis Isat Falls in Ethiopia, Blue Nile Falls flow down a chasm near Lake Tana, the source of the Blue Nile River.

1) The Land

Ethiopia lies in northeastern Africa, in a region known as the Horn of Africa. Occupying an area of 426,373 square miles, Ethiopia is larger than the states of Texas and New Mexico combined. Roughly triangular in shape, it is bordered by Sudan in the west, Kenya in the south, Djibouti and the Red Sea in the northeast, Somalia in the southeast, and the newly independent Eritrea in the north.

Boundaries

Ethiopia's border with Sudan, one of the longest boundaries on the African continent, was created in 1902. This international boundary cuts through the mountainous western highlands of Ethiopia. In the southwest the border is defined by the Akobo River, which eventually joins the White Nile in southern Sudan.

The nation's boundary with Djibouti came into being in 1935 as a result of a territorial agreement between France and Italy, which ruled the two African countries at the time. Ethiopia's southern border with Kenya was established in the 1950s in cooperation with Great Britain, Kenya's colonial power until its independence in 1964.

Similarly, the border between Ethiopia and Somalia was defined by a loose agreement established between 1897 and 1908 among Italy, Great Britain, and Ethiopia. The United Nations redefined the boundary in 1950. In the past three decades, Ethiopia has experienced more disputes with Somalia regarding their mutual boundary than it has with any of its other neighbors. Somalia's belief in the concept of a greater Somalia—one nation for all people of Somali heritage who live on the Horn of Africa (including the Ogaden region of eastern Ethiopia)—has been one of the motives behind the continuous border conflicts.

Ethiopia has been a landlocked country since 1993, when the province of Eritrea gained its formal independence. The loss of its ports on the Red Sea, an important international shipping route, was a severe blow to Ethiopia, which depends on the shipment of food and other supplies to relieve its famine-stricken areas. However, Ethiopia and Eritrea have agreed to keep the Red Sea port of Assab open to Ethiopian trade shipments.

Courtesy of American Lutheran Church

In desert regions of the country, people travel barefoot over long stretches of hot sand.

Courtesy of J. Bland, WHO Photo

Cattle gather at a small stream that supports vegetation and animal life in a narrow Ethiopian valley.

Topography

Two landscape features—an elevated central plateau and a north-south section of the Great Rift Valley, which splits the plateau into western and eastern parts—dominate Ethiopia's topography. Lowlands occupy much of southern Ethiopia. The plateaus—coupled with the southern lowlands—make up two-thirds of the nation's territory.

Although Ethiopia's central feature is called a plateau, it is a rugged piece of territory interrupted by small, fertile tablelands, which are often used for growing grain and grazing cattle. The western section of the central plateau, sometimes called the Amhara Plateau, has heights of 10,000 to 15,000 feet. The Simyen Mountains rise in this area and include Ras

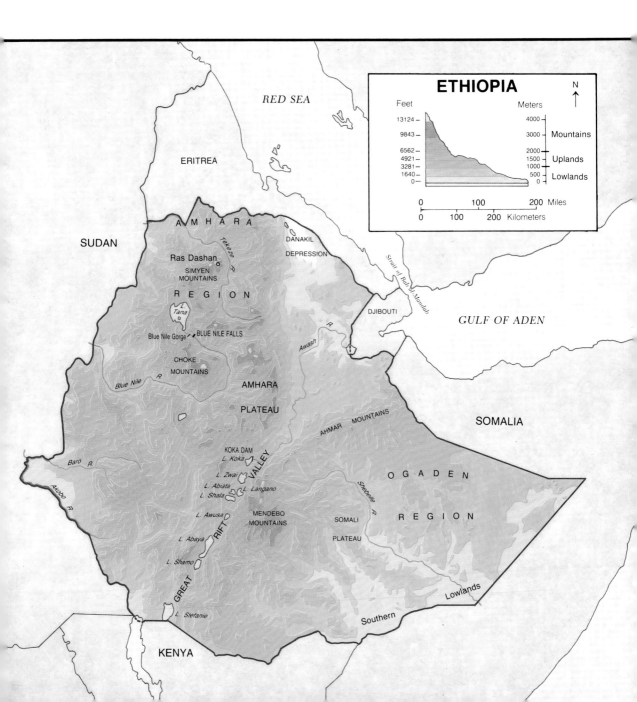

The Great Rift Valley stretches from the Middle East to Mozambique. In Ethiopia the valley's terrain is mountainous and lush with plant life.

Dashan (15,158 feet), the nation's highest peak. The Amhara Plateau receives adequate rain for farming without irrigation and, therefore, has greater agricultural potential than Ethiopia's other plateaus. The Choke Mountains, another major range, lie north and west of the capital city of Addis Ababa.

To the east of the Great Rift Valley is the continuation of the central plateau, known as the Somali Plateau. It includes mountains, such as the Mendebo and Ahmar ranges, and desert—the semi-arid Ogaden region. Lower in elevation, the eastern plateau has been the scene of a long border dispute with Somalia, which hopes to acquire the Ogaden. In the 1980s, famine and refugee problems created misery for the residents of this region.

THE GREAT RIFT VALLEY

Stretching from the Middle East to southeastern Africa, the Great Rift Valley is a fault in the earth's crust that was formed by volcanic action or by earthquakes. In the southern portion of Ethiopia, the Rift Valley becomes a deep trench that cuts through the central plateau from northeast to southwest. This valley also includes the Danakil Depression, a large triangular desert that crosses the border between Ethiopia and Eritrea. Sections of the depression are 300 feet below sea level and record some of the hottest temperatures in the world.

Rivers and Lakes

The Abbai (Blue Nile), the most notable of Ethiopia's rivers and the chief tributary of the Nile, originates in Lake Tana in north central Ethiopia. The Abbai flows through the western section of the central plateau to join the White Nile in Khartoum, Sudan. The Blue Nile, the Tekeze, and the Baro, which all contribute to the Nile,

The Blue Nile—also known as the Abbai River—flows from Lake Tana through the highlands of Ethiopia to Khartoum, the capital city of Sudan. The length of the river's course is 850 miles.

Courtesy of Carl Purcell, Eliot Elisofon Archives, National Museum of African Art, Smithsonian Institution

account for about half of the outflow of water from Ethiopia. Other major rivers include the Awash, which flows into a series of small lakes in the eastern lowlands, and the Shebelle, which cuts through the southeastern portion of the country and goes into Somalia.

Lake Tana, the largest freshwater lake in Ethiopia, is situated in the heart of the central highlands. Roughly square in shape, the lake covers an area of about 1,100 square miles. A chain of lakes—Koka, Zwai, Langano, Abiata, Shala, Awusa, Abaya, and Shamo—lie close to one another in the Great Rift Valley. Some of them are freshwater lakes and, therefore, are dependent on small rivers feeding into them. Others receive their large volume of water from hot, underground springs containing various salts and minerals.

Courtesy of American Lutheran Church

A narrowing of the Blue Nile's course—caught between steep walls of rock—is known as Blue Nile Gorge.

Courtesy of Tony Fennerty, M.D., and Bogdan Szajkowski, Ph.D.

Sailors paddle boats made of papyrus, a tall marsh grass, to visit settlements that line the shores of Lake Tana.

13

Ethiopians gather at one of the country's several crater lakes to attend a religious ceremony.

Throughout Ethiopia's varied landscape—but particularly in hot, dry areas—camels provide reliable transport.

Climate

Changes in Ethiopia's climate do not necessarily depend on changes in season. Instead, differences in elevation produce variations in temperature ranging from cool to temperate to hot. These variations are known to Ethiopians as *dega, weina dega,* and *kolla,* respectively.

The cool zone (dega) consists of the central and eastern plateaus, which have elevations above 7,000 feet. Temperatures in this zone range from 60° F to the freezing point. Summerlike temperatures occur during the months of March, April, and May.

The temperate region (weina dega) is a pleasant place to live and a productive place to farm. This climatic zone covers much of the highland region and is densely populated. Altitudes range from 5,000 to 7,000 feet, and temperatures vary between 60° F and 85° F.

A cluster of round dwellings lies amid sparse woods in an elevated region of Ethiopia.

Livestock graze in one of the well-watered valleys of the highlands.

15

The hot zone (kolla) includes the Danakil Depression and nearby lowlands, the eastern Ogaden, and the deep valleys of the Abbai River. These regions are less than 5,000 feet above sea level. The climatic conditions are uncomfortably hot throughout the year, and the temperature varies from 85° F to as much as 122° F in some places.

In addition to different climatic zones, Ethiopia has two identifiable seasons. The dry season occurs from mid-September through May, and the rainy season takes place during the months of June, July, and August. Average annual rainfall varies according to elevation, with higher areas generally being wetter. Addis Ababa, situated in the mountains, gets about 43 inches a year. Rainfall is less in the plains and river valleys. Desert areas like the Ogaden and parts of the Danakil Depression are the driest regions, receiving from 0 to 8 inches annually.

Courtesy of Ethiopian Tourism Commission

Rare walia ibex, agile members of the goat family, live in mountainous areas of Ethiopia—the only country where the wild species is found.

Wildlife

Ethiopia boasts a variety of wildlife. Most of the familiar African mammals—elephants, zebras, giraffes, lions, leopards, antelope, rhinoceroses, hyenas, and baboons—live there. Hippopotamuses and crocodiles inhabit lakes and rivers, and reptiles and fish abound. In the Great Rift Valley, game fowl—such as cuckoos, weaverbirds, hawks, eagles, flamingos, and flycatchers—are plentiful. In the Simyen Mountains, walia ibex—mountain goats found only in Ethiopia—roam freely.

An animal of considerable economic value is the civet cat, a mammal with long, gray hair and spots and bands on its back. The civet cat has glands near its tail where a musky substance, similar to that found in the skunk, is produced. This substance, called civet, has an unpleasant smell but nevertheless is highly prized as an ingredient in the making of perfumes. Ethiopia is the world's chief supplier of this product, which captures and retains delicate fragrances.

Courtesy of Tony Fennerty, M.D., and Bogdan Szajkowski, Ph.D.

Women carry firewood across a stone bridge in Gojam province in western Ethiopia.

Courtesy of Agency for International Development

Some of Ethiopia's vegetation reflect the hardy traits—such as thick leaves and long roots—that characterize desert plants.

Vegetation

In the past two decades, Ethiopia—like most African nations—has encountered the problem of dwindling forests, a result of using large quantities of wood for both construction and fuel. Although minor efforts to reforest have begun, Ethiopia continues to struggle against environmental problems that arise from deforestation. For example, after centuries of clearing the land, the desert is expanding in the north and in other semi-arid areas. Moreover, continual erosion of topsoil occurs from heavy rainfall as well as from tropical winds.

The lowlands along the international boundaries of the east and the northeast are semidesert or desert regions, with little or no rain throughout the year. The terrain is dotted with bushy growth, interrupted only by an occasional acacia tree. A common plant is sansevieria, popular as a houseplant in Great Britain and the United States, where it is often called a snake plant.

Temperate-zone forests and high mountain vegetation cover the Amhara Plateau of the northwest and the Somali Plateau of the southeast. Eucalyptus—a tree imported from Australia—grows around Addis Ababa and other cities. The tree's root system, which develops quickly and holds the soil together, helps to control erosion.

Natural Resources

The mineral resources of Ethiopia have not been fully investigated. So far, gold and platinum are the only metals of economic value that have been mined. Surveys made when Italy occupied the nation in the 1930s, as well as those made in recent years, indicate the presence of copper, lead, magnesium, and iron. Deposits of clay and limestone are common, but they support only a modest amount of brick

17

and cement manufacturing. Extensive salt deposits also exist, and recent studies indicate that petroleum deposits lie off the coast of the Red Sea and that potash is available in the Danakil region.

Cities

Only 15 percent of Ethiopia's total population reside in urban areas. The rest live in rural parts of the country, although famine and civil strife have caused more rural inhabitants to move to the cities.

ADDIS ABABA

Addis Ababa means "New Flower" in Amharic, and the city was founded in 1887 by Sahle Mariam, the man who would become Emperor Menelik II. Capital of Ethiopia since 1896, the city is also the headquarters of the United Nations Economic Commission for Africa and as the seat of the Organization of African Unity (OAU). Indeed, the OAU charter was negotiated at a meeting in Addis Ababa's Africa Hall.

Broad avenues crisscross the sprawling capital, whose population nearly doubled between 1960 and 1970. Situated in the heart of Shewa province, Addis Ababa has a current population of more than 1.6 million. The city is 8,200 feet above sea level, which gives it a springlike climate throughout the year. Modern buildings stand side by side with traditional mud homes, and the city's Mercato has a reputation as the biggest open-air market in Africa.

SECONDARY URBAN CENTERS

Other important urban centers are scattered throughout the country. Dese, the capital of Welo province in north central Ethiopia, has a population of about 76,000. In the southeast lies Harer (population 63,000), which is in an important coffee-growing region. Debre Markos (population 40,000), the main city in Gojam province, is situated on an all-weather road about 110 miles northwest of Addis Ababa. In all three of these cities, population has been

Photo by Robert Caputo

A wide street in Addis Ababa, the capital of Ethiopia, leads to City Hall—the administrative headquarters of the city.

18

Photo by Robert Caputo

Asmara, the main city of Eritrea, lies at an altitude of 7,765 feet above sea level. Before the Italian invasion of the late nineteenth century, the city was a small farming settlement.

Photo by Robert Caputo

A banner picturing three famous Marxist thinkers—Karl Marx, Frederich Engels, and V. I. Lenin—is the backdrop for a crowd gathered in Addis Ababa for May Day celebrations in 1982.

Carved from a single piece of stone, a stela (pillar) at the ancient site of Aksum probably fell during its construction roughly 1,500 years ago.

Gonder, the capital of Ethiopia from the seventeenth to the nineteenth centuries, became a center of religion, art, and learning.

Castles—the work of successive Ethiopian emperors—dot Gonder's landscape.

declining since the 1980s, despite an influx of refugees from the war-torn countryside.

Aksum (population 12,000) was an imperial city in the early Christian era during the height of the Aksumite kingdom. Crowning ceremonies of Ethiopian emperors took place in Aksum until the Middle Ages. Beautiful tombs, some of which are giant stelae (upright stone slabs), hold the remains of ancient kings. Ancient peoples believed that the stelae represented the gateway through which the soul of the deceased person traveled to the afterworld.

From the seventeenth to the nineteenth centuries, Gonder (population 95,000)—located about 20 miles north of Lake Tana—was Ethiopia's capital. During the reigns of the seventeenth-century Emperor Fasilides and his successors, many castles, palaces, and fortifications were built. Not only are there castles in Gonder, but the city has several beautiful churches, which managed to survive the destruction of several invading armies.

Asmara (population 296,000), once Ethiopia's largest urban center, is now the largest city of Eritrea. Highways and a railroad link the city with the port of Mesewa on the Red Sea. Set amid rich farmlands at an altitude of over 7,000 feet, Asmara is a handsome city with many impressive, Italian-style public buildings. In recent times, a university and an army training complex have been added to the city's landmarks.

Wearing a traditional garment called a *shamma*, an Ethiopian priest stands in front of the Cathedral of St. Mary of Zion in Aksum.

Heavily decorated pillars stand in Aksum, the main site of the Aksumite kingdom that flourished from the fourth through the seventh centuries A.D. Scientists disagree on the function of the pillars, but most believe them to be tombs or commemorative markers.

2) History and Government

Archaeological findings reveal that human ancestors lived in Ethiopia two million years ago. The known history of Ethiopia began when immigrants from Saba, a kingdom in southern Arabia, crossed the Red Sea sometime between 2000 and 1000 B.C.

The Sabeans spoke Semitic languages, which today are represented by Arabic, Hebrew, and several Ethiopian languages, such as Amharic and Tigrinya. Settling along the coast, the Sabeans eventually moved inland to the highland of Tigre and Eritrea, where they came into contact with the Cushitic-speakers who already lived in the area. A mixed Semitic-Cushitic people emerged from this encounter, and by the first century A.D. they had formed a kingdom whose capital was at Aksum.

Ethiopians claim that the now-deposed royal line sprang from the union of the queen of Sheba (Sheba is another form of the word Saba) and King Solomon of Israel. In 980 B.C. Maqeda, the queen of

Sheba, decided to lead an expedition to the court of King Solomon. Attracted by her beauty, the king tricked the queen into a sexual encounter, which produced a child who ascended the throne of his mother as Menelik I. Thus, according to tradition, he became the first of a long line of Ethiopian emperors descended from Solomon.

The Aksumite Kingdom

At its height from the fourth to the seventh centuries A.D., the Aksumite kingdom covered most of present-day Eritrea, Tigre, and Welo. In Adulis, Aksum's port (near modern Mesewa), Egyptian sailors, Syrian traders, and East Indian merchants bartered for gold, copper, olive oil, utensils, and spices. Aksum also conducted a brisk trade in ivory and rhinoceros horn.

King Ezana, who reigned in the fourth century and who proved to be a strong leader, was converted to Christianity by missionaries from Syria. Eventually, the king's subjects also adopted the new religion. Christianity influenced the development of religious art, music, and literature. The latter was written in Geez, which is still used in Ethiopian Christian rites and which is the forerunner of modern Ethiopian languages.

The power of the Aksumite kingdom began to wane in the seventh century. At that time armies of Arabs—who followed the faith of Islam and were called Muslims—gained control of Arabia, the Red Sea, and northern Africa. This event ended the long cultural contact between Christian countries and Ethiopia, which, thereafter, was cut off from the rest of the Christian world by 1,000 miles of Muslim territory. As a result, the kingdom's trade with Europe largely ended.

A thirteenth-century French statue depicts the queen of Sheba, or Saba, whose lands were located in the southern Arabian Peninsula, probably near present-day Yemen.

23

Pushed out of northern Ethiopia by Muslim armies, the Aksumite kingdom tried to reestablish itself farther south. It failed in its efforts to acquire small kingdoms in the heartland of present-day Ethiopia and to convert the peoples there to Christianity. Meanwhile, the Muslim armies were again on the move. By the tenth century, the Aksumite kingdom had lost all of its lands to Islamic conquest.

Return of the Solomonic Line

In the 1130s a new line of Christian kings —the Zagwe—established itself in Ethiopia. A Cushitic people, the Zagwe came from the Lasta Mountains. They founded their capital at Roha (modern Lalibela) and dotted the landscape there with churches and monasteries. Unlike the Aksumite kingdom, the Zagwe dynasty could not claim royal descent from Solomon and Sheba (called the Solomonic line). The

Courtesy of Donald Crummey

The rough stone churches at Lalibela are known for their carved architectural details.

Courtesy of Donald Crummey

By digging deep trenches around huge slabs of volcanic rock, builders at Lalibela created churches of solid design that were hard to reach. The inaccessibility of the holy places suggests the threat to the Christian religion in Ethiopia from the attacks of Muslim armies.

A colorful fresco, or painting on plaster, depicts a biblical scene and decorates a fourteenth-century church on the island of Kebrane Gabriel in Lake Tana.

Ethiopian Orthodox Church, along with remnants—such as the Amhara and the Tigre peoples—of the former Aksumite kingdom came to regard a connection with the Solomonic line as the only legitimate link to the Ethiopian throne.

In 1270 Yekuno Amlaq, an Amhara prince, overthrew the Zagwe and reestablished the Solomonic dynasty. The center of the reborn kingdom was the Amhara region. Yekuno Amlaq and his successors extended this region to include many Muslim territories, such as Gojam and Gonder. Zera Yaqob, a ruthless though efficient Ethiopian king, ruled from 1434 to 1468. Militarily, he managed to defeat or limit the power of smaller, surrounding realms. More importantly, he achieved needed political and church reforms.

More Muslim Invaders

After the fall of Zera Yaqob in 1468, the Ethiopian monarchy had difficulties deter-mining who would be the ruler. Because of this instability, an opportunity opened up for another wave of Muslim invasions of Christian Ethiopia.

Raids and counter-raids went on between Christians and Muslims until the leader of the Muslim armies, Ahmad ibn Ibrahim al-Ghazi, waged a jihad (holy war) to break Christian rule in Ethiopia. As a popular military chief and strong religious leader, al-Ghazi attracted a large following. In 1529 the Muslim forces dramatically defeated the Christian troops of the Ethiopian emperor Lebna Dengel. The victors took prisoners, burned churches, and continued to march toward the interior. Eventually, they penetrated the heartland of the Ethiopian Empire—the Amhara region.

In 1543 with military support requested from Portugal—with whom Ethiopia had recently made contact—the Ethiopian emperor Gelawdewos captured and killed al-Ghazi. This event was a permanent blow to Muslim power in Ethiopia.

Contact with Europe

The renewal of contact with Europe in the sixteenth century shifted Ethiopia from a period of isolation to one of participation in the world scene. Indeed, the name Abyssinia, long used by Europeans to denote Ethiopia, dates from this period and is a variation of Al-Habesha, the name of an area near the coast of the Red Sea.

Relations with Portugal, however, were marred by the activities of Portuguese missionaries. These Europeans sought to convert Ethiopians from the Ethiopian Orthodox Church to Roman Catholicism. Emperor Fasilides came to power in 1632, when his Roman Catholic father gave up the throne to end the religious infighting between those who supported Roman Catholicism and those who belonged to the Ethiopian Church. In 1633 the new emperor expelled the Catholic missionaries. Thereafter, Ethiopia maintained a more distant relationship with Europe until the nineteenth century, when Great Britain opened a diplomatic office in Ethiopia in 1805.

The era of the princes began in the mid-1700s and lasted for more than 100 years. The emperor's centralized authority gave way to the power of independent regional rulers, each of whom controlled a specific area. Civil wars were common during this chaotic period.

Tewodros II

Among the warring princes was Lij Kassa, who succeeded in establishing his power over most of the country. He was crowned emperor in 1855, taking the name of Tewodros II. Sahle Mariam had been heir to the Ethiopian throne when Tewodros took it. The new emperor put the heir in prison, but Sahle Mariam escaped in 1865 and joined a rebel group that actively opposed the Tewodros regime.

In 1867 Tewodros imprisoned several British citizens, people whom the emperor

In the seventeenth century, when Christian missionary activity resumed in Ethiopia, a monastery — or religious household — was established near Lake Tana. A fresco from the monastery's church shows the enthronement of Jesus.

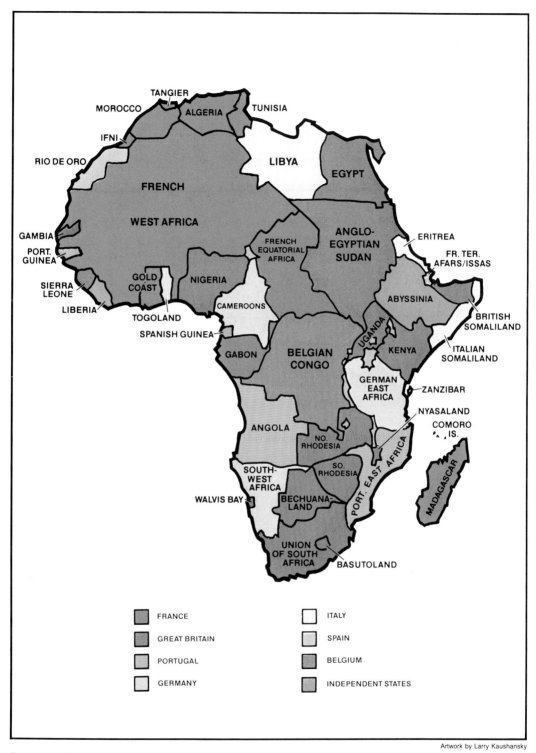

TANGIER
MOROCCO
ALGERIA
TUNISIA
IFNI
RIO DE ORO
LIBYA
EGYPT
FRENCH
WEST AFRICA
GAMBIA
PORT.
GUINEA
FRENCH
EQUATORIAL
AFRICA
ANGLO-
EGYPTIAN
SUDAN
ERITREA
FR. TER.
AFARS/ISSAS
SIERRA
LEONE
GOLD
COAST
NIGERIA
ABYSSINIA
LIBERIA
CAMEROONS
BRITISH
SOMALILAND
TOGOLAND
SPANISH GUINEA
UGANDA
KENYA
ITALIAN
SOMALILAND
GABON
BELGIAN
CONGO
GERMAN
EAST
AFRICA
ZANZIBAR
NYASALAND
COMORO
IS.
ANGOLA
NO.
RHODESIA
SOUTH-
WEST
AFRICA
SO.
RHODESIA
PORT. EAST AFRICA
MADAGASCAR
WALVIS BAY
BECHUANA-
LAND
UNION
OF SOUTH
AFRICA
BASUTOLAND

FRANCE
GREAT BRITAIN
PORTUGAL
GERMANY
ITALY
SPAIN
BELGIUM
INDEPENDENT STATES

Artwork by Larry Kaushansky

Europeans referred to Ethiopia as Abyssinia, which was taken from Al-Habesha, an area along the Red Sea. After nineteenth-century European powers divided the continent into spheres of influence, Abyssinia became the only independent kingdom on the continent. (Liberia was an independent republic.) Map information taken from *The Anchor Atlas of World History*, 1978.

Courtesy of James H. Marrinan

Minted in Paris in the 1890s, an Ethiopian coin shows the crowned head of the emperor Menelik II *(top)* and the lion of Judah *(bottom).* The lion symbolizes the royal claim of being descended from Solomon, king of Judah.

During this period, however, the empire lost its access to the sea when Italy took over Eritrea. Nevertheless, the empire's other borders were recognized by European powers and remained intact despite the scramble for colonies that dominated Africa in the late nineteenth century.

In addition to establishing Addis Ababa as the empire's capital, Menelik also expanded the imperial boundaries to nearly double their original size. Superior firepower and a good military organization brought Menelik success in subduing regions in the south and southwest.

The Italians

Like other European powers in the late nineteenth century, Italy was determined to secure territories in Africa. The Italians focused their colonial desires on northeastern Africa, particularly on Ethiopia. In 1890 the Treaty of Uccialli was negotiated between Italy and Ethiopia. Two copies of the treaty were prepared, one in Amharic —the Ethiopian language—and the other in Italian. On the strength of the Italian version, Francesco Crispi, the prime minister of Italy, made it known to all European countries that Ethiopia had been made a protectorate of Italy. The European powers adjusted their maps accordingly.

When Menelik II discovered the misunderstanding, he protested immediately. The wording of the treaty in Amharic gave the emperor the right to ask for help from Italy in times of need, but the treaty did not make Ethiopia a territory of Italy. Menelik II at once wrote to Britain's Queen Victoria, to the ruler of Germany, and to the president of France, insisting that Ethiopia was still an independent nation. In 1893 he denounced the treaty, and by 1895 Ethiopia and Italy were at war.

In March 1896 Menelik's troops defeated the Italian army of about 15,000 soldiers at Adwa. Italy later negotiated a treaty recognizing Ethiopia's indepen-

suspected of plotting against him. As a result, the British sent troops to Ethiopia in 1868. The rebels, who had murdered two of Tewodros's advisers, joined the British. In the battle that followed, Tewodros was defeated, after which he took his own life. Disorder prevailed until 1872, when the ruler of Tigre province proclaimed himself Emperor John IV. When John IV died in battle, Sahle Mariam took the throne as Menelik II and began the history of modern Ethiopia.

Menelik II

Menelik II ruled from 1889 to 1913 and was able to impose some control over the frequently warring regions of Ethiopia.

dence but remained in Eritrea until the middle of the Second World War.

The Early Twentieth Century

Menelik died in 1913, and his chosen successor was deposed in 1916. Thereafter, his daughter Zauditu ruled as empress. Her cousin Ras Tafari, Menelik's grandnephew, was proclaimed Zauditu's heir and successor. Conflicts arose between the empress and her cousin, and by 1928 Ras Tafari had emerged as the stronger of the two relations. The empress died in 1930, and on November 2 of that year Ras Tafari was crowned emperor under the name Haile Selassie.

Haile Selassie was the 225th successor of the Solomonic dynasty. The name Haile Selassie means "the Power of the Trinity" in Amharic, and his official titles also included "King of Kings" and "the Lion of Judah." Seven months after his ascension to the throne in 1930, Haile Selassie decreed the nation's first written constitution. Through his efforts, Ethiopia became a member of an international organization called the League of Nations in 1932.

The new emperor spent the first half of the 1930s strengthening his authority within the country. During the latter half of the decade, he was in exile in Great Britain after an Italian invasion forced him to flee.

Courtesy of Jeannine Bayard

One of the traditional titles of Ethiopian monarchs was "Conquering Lion of the Tribe of Judah." During Haile Selassie's reign, a statue of the lion in Addis Ababa represented the 225 successive rulers who had claimed the title.

In a period cartoon of the 1930s, European diplomats give weak assurances to Haile Selassie about Italy's designs on Ethiopian territory.

The Second Italian Invasion

Beginning in 1889, the Italians had occupied most of the Somali coast and had retained control of Eritrea. But the boundary between Italy's colonies and Ethiopia was in dispute, and in 1934 shots were exchanged across the border. After peace attempts broke down, the Italians entered Ethiopia. By 1936 they had conquered the entire country.

Haile Selassie asked the League of Nations to support the security of the Ethiopian Empire. Nevertheless, both France and Great Britain—who wanted to avoid conflicts that might lead to war—recognized Italy's control of Ethiopia. In addition, the league voted not to impose any penalties on Italy. The only major powers who refused to acknowledge Italy's posi-

tion were the United States and the Soviet Union.

During World War II (1939–1945), Haile Selassie, with British and Ethiopian troops, overthrew the forces of the Italian dictator Benito Mussolini. Arriving in Addis Ababa in 1941, exactly five years after he had left the capital, the emperor soon regained authority throughout most of the nation.

Eritrea governed itself under British protection until the United Nations made the area part of Ethiopia in 1952. Ethiopia claimed Eritrea as a province—to be administered by the central Ethiopian government—in 1962. Yet the Eritreans never accepted rule by Ethiopia, and the situation led to a guerrilla war that lasted from the 1960s until the 1990s.

Haile Selassie

Although a firm believer in his divine right to rule, Haile Selassie was also a political realist. He knew that his desire to modernize the country would only serve to alienate Ethiopia's traditional nobility. The emperor's policies, therefore, did not reduce the privileges of the wealthy. He did manage, however, to reform the Ethiopian Orthodox Church and to centralize administrative power.

Haile Selassie attempted to introduce changes while at the same time preserving his traditional powers. The two efforts, however, created conflict among those around him. In 1960, while the emperor was abroad, several groups—mostly of the military—joined to lead a coup d'état. Large numbers of university students supported the coup, which was aimed at improving the position of ordinary Ethiopians. Despite its popular goals, the coup attempt failed—mainly because the air force and army remained loyal to the emperor. Nevertheless, the coup shattered the view that the monarch was universally accepted.

Courtesy of Donald Crummey

Emperor Haile Selassie I ruled as regent during a transition period from 1916 to 1930 and as emperor from 1930 to 1974.

Courtesy of American Lutheran Church

As one of Africa's oldest leaders, Haile Selassie *(back row)* put forth an image of experience, moderation, and strength. Here, he participates in a meeting of Lutheran ministers in Africa in 1965.

Signs of Dissatisfaction

By the late 1960s and early 1970s, signs of dissatisfaction became more apparent. In 1967 rural workers rose up in Gojam to demand land reform. University students led demonstrations for less censorship and especially for a speeding-up of political and social changes. The Eritrean Liberation Front (ELF) led guerrilla fighters in Eritrea and began a major campaign of armed struggle that caused the government to declare a state of emergency in most of the area.

In the early 1970s famine spread across northern and eastern Ethiopia. Because the emperor feared that the disaster might damage his overseas reputation, he chose not to tell the international community about the ravaging hunger in his realm. As a result, 300,000 people died of famine in 11 regions. Not until November 1973 did the emperor allow international agencies to engage in emergency relief operations. The emperor's mishandling of the famine disaster caused considerable unrest and was one of the reasons for his overthrow a year later.

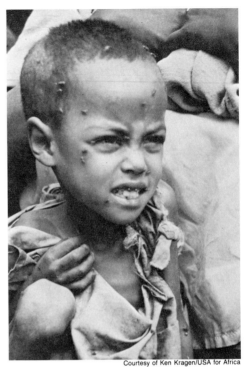

The famine crises of the 1970s and 1980s affected the health and caused the deaths of hundreds of thousands of Ethiopians.

Change of Political Direction

In September 1974 a military declaration abolished the monarchy. After 44 years of complete power, Emperor Haile Selassie was driven out of the palace grounds in an old Volkswagen. Soon after his loss of power, Haile Selassie died while in the custody of the new government. Because the emperor had cultivated an image abroad as one of Africa's reliable and experienced leaders, his death was a great shock to the international community. But within Ethiopia—because of the nation's internal problems—his exit from power excited different emotions.

On September 12, 1975, a group of military officers, calling themselves a Derg, or committee, declared Ethiopia to be a socialist state. They described their group as a provisional military government.

International agencies distributed dried milk to thousands of mothers and children during the famine of the early 1970s.

In general, Ethiopia's farming techniques are simple and time-consuming. The Derg attempted to introduce more modern methods and formed farming cooperatives throughout the country.

Photo by Phil Porter

After the declaration, conflicts emerged within the Derg, and several members of the ruling committee, including two of its chairmen, were executed. In 1976 Major (now Lieutenant Colonel) Mengistu Haile-Mariam became the unchallenged leader of the government.

Holding strong socialist beliefs, Mengistu turned away from the West and sought to ally Ethiopia with Communist countries, such as the Soviet Union and Cuba. His regime steadily became more authoritarian, stamping out political opposition and eliminating public dissent.

Courtesy of American Lutheran Church

Land reform is a major issue in modern Ethiopia. Much of the land seized by the Mengistu government has remained in the hands of rural cooperatives. Most Ethiopians live in rural clusters, sometimes in round dwellings near small plots of land, which they cultivate to provide food for their families.

33

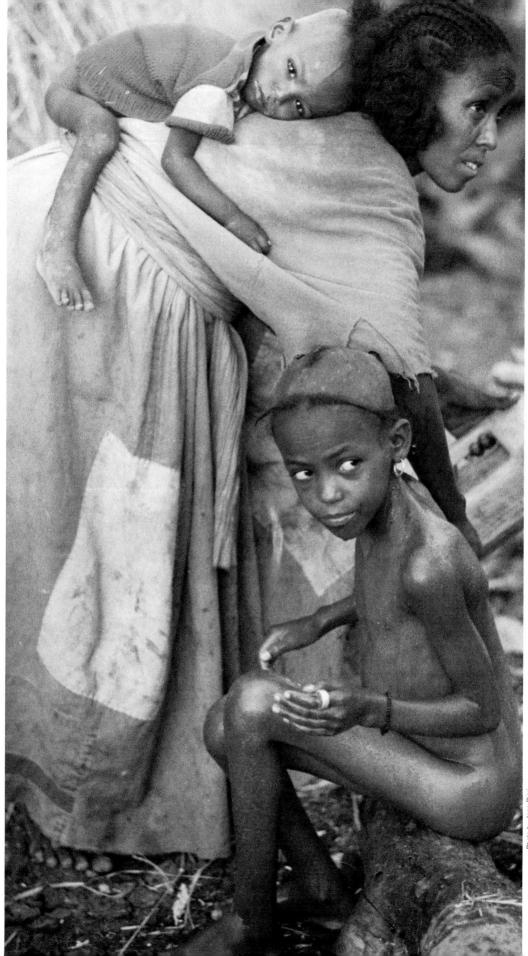

Famine has struck Ethiopia several times since the 1970s. Seeking food and escape from war-torn areas, a woman and her two children *(opposite)* wait in a Sudanese refugee camp. Within Ethiopia, villagers *(above)* in Harer province line up to receive food.

The Politics of Famine

Chronic drought and erosion resulting from overgrazing and deforestation have limited the ability of Ethiopia's people to feed themselves. As a result, famine has struck Ethiopia several times in the last three decades. The government's response —both under the monarchy and the Derg—often has depended on political factors. For example, in the early 1970s, Haile Selassie refused to publicize the Eritrean famine because it would have negatively affected his image abroad.

After the 1974 coup, famine again became a news item. This time, however, the government sought and welcomed overseas help, including the efforts of worldwide campaigns such as Live Aid and USA for Africa. Nevertheless, Ethiopian officials hampered the efforts of international agencies to deliver relief supplies, especially to war-torn areas of northern Ethiopia such as Eritrea and Tigre. In 1987 guerrillas in favor of self-government for Eritrea destroyed trucks and food supplies that were on their way to relief camps in the region.

In addition, Ethiopia's poor transportation system has often prevented food from arriving where it is most needed. Docking space for grain-laden ships is unavailable, and vessels wait for days to unload. Once unloaded, grain waits at dockside—occasionally until it rots—for trucks (also in short supply) that will distribute it. Even then, the roads used to carry relief supplies may be impassable.

In the mid-1980s, the Mengistu government began a resettlement program aimed at relocating refugees into areas that were less affected by famine and that had agricultural potential. The program's goal was to resettle 30 million rural people into villages made up of collectivized (jointly run) farms.

Of 600,000 refugees who were forcibly relocated to the south in 1986, about 100,000 died en route to the new areas. Critics of the program claimed that the southern lands, though more fertile and less densely populated, are disease-ridden. The fall of the Mengistu regime put an end to the project.

Overthrow of Mengistu

Until the late 1970s, the ELF was the main movement dedicated to the liberation of Eritrea from the control of the Ethiopian government. The movement began in 1961 as a response to a United Nations resolution that combined Eritrea with Ethiopia.

Ideological and ethnic conflicts resulted in a split within the ELF. As a result, a more radical faction, known as the Eritrean People's Liberation Front (EPLF), formed in 1970. In 1978 the Ethiopian government, backed by weapons and advisers supplied by the Soviet Union and Cuba, launched a major attack that dealt the ELF a crippling blow. Its surviving troops joined the EPLF, which emerged as the sole independence movement within Eritrea in the 1980s.

At the same time, the continuing fighting was weakening the Ethiopian army. During a rebel attack in May 1991, Mengistu suddenly fled Addis Ababa. Resistance in the capital collapsed, and the well-organized Ethiopian People's Revolutionary Democratic Front (EPRDF) took power. Meles Zenawi, the leader of the EPRDF, became Ethiopia's provisional president.

Somali soldiers try to repair a Soviet-built tank, which was abandoned by Ethiopian troops fighting in border wars near Harer, eastern Ethiopia.

Photo by Andrew E. Beswick

Seated between United Nations diplomats, President Meles Zenawi hosts a 1992 conference on Somalia. After coming to power, Zenawi led a regional attempt to resolve the Somalian civil war.

Zenawi arranged a conference in July, to which the country's many rebel factions sent representatives. The conference established an interim government and planned nationwide, free elections to take place in 1994. A new legislature, made up of several rival political groups, began meeting in Addis Ababa.

The defeat of Mengistu encouraged the independence movement in Eritrea, which was no longer opposed by the Ethiopian army. In the spring of 1993, the Eritreans voted overwhelmingly for self-rule. The province was quickly recognized as an independent country by the United Nations. The leaders of the EPLF guerrillas control Eritrea's government.

Courtesy of Agency for International Development

Mass migrations have resulted from the ethnic conflicts taking place in many regions of Ethiopia.

During the 1993 referendum on Eritrean independence, Eritrean voters living in Addis Ababa proudly display their new national identity cards.

By the late 1990s, Ethiopia had begun to recover from the many years of civil war and famine. The EPRDF leadership, made up mostly of an ethnic group known as Tigrayans, allowed more independence to other ethnic groups and granted them self-determination in their own regions. The Ethiopian economy also began to recover, with several foreign nations investing directly in Ethiopian businesses.

For the first time in many years, Ethiopia allows competing political parties to take part in the central government. Nevertheless the EPRDF party holds an overwhelming majority in the legislature, making Ethiopia still, in effect, a one-party state. In addition the central government has banned some militant rival political groups. Ethnic rivalry continues to strain the country's political scene.

Government

After the defeat of the Mengistu government, a conference of rebel groups in Addis

A statue of V. I. Lenin, founder of the Soviet Union's Communist party, stood prominently in Addis Ababa during the 1980s.

Ababa formed a transitional government. The government drafted a new constitution providing for nine states, seven of which are based on a dominant ethnic group. Each group may form its own political parties to govern in its particular state. These states also may secede by holding a referendum, although the central government actively opposes all calls for secession.

The Ethiopian legislature consists of a 548-member Council of People's Representatives and a 117-member Federal Council. After legislative elections in 1995, the EPRDF held a total of 593 seats in both houses.

The Ethiopian legislature elects a president to serve as Ethiopia's head of state. The prime minister, however, has more direct control over the functions of government. The prime minister also heads a cabinet of 16 officials who run the various government ministries. In local matters, district councils and neighborhood committees make decisions.

A supreme court sits in Addis Ababa and is divided into civil, criminal, and military sections. A high court hears appeals on civil and criminal cases from provincial courts, which include *awraja* (regional) and *warada* (local) courts.

In peaceful areas of Ethiopia, peasant associations have sponsored campaigns to improve health conditions. Here, a nurse visits a rural village.

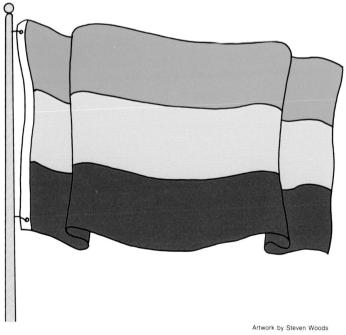

The Derg chose to retain Ethiopia's flag, which has been in use since the late nineteenth century. The flag's colors—green, yellow, and red—have come to be known as Pan-African but, in Ethiopia, they had an early connection to the Christian idea of the Trinity. A more recent interpretation claims that green represents the earth, that yellow stands for natural resources, and that red symbolizes national courage.

Although 12 percent of Ethiopia's children die before they reach the age of 5, nearly half of the nation's population is under the age of 15.

3) The People

Ethiopia has 58.7 million people, most of whom live in rural areas. With a current population growth rate of 2.8 percent, it is estimated that the number of Ethiopians will double in 25 years. This prospect makes the government's attempts to improve health care and to wipe out famine even more pressing.

Ethnic Mixture

Ethiopia's people belong to many ethnic groups and have distinct linguistic backgrounds. The nation's ethnic groups are classified according to the languages they speak. Seventy known languages exist, but Amharic has emerged as the national form of communication. This choice shows the historical dominance of the Amharas and also recognizes their strong written tradition.

Nevertheless, the largest ethnic group in Ethiopia is the Oromo, who are found in the western, southern, and southeastern parts of the country. Tigre-speaking people of the north comprise approximately 20 percent of the Ethiopian population. Other ethnic groups include the Gurage, who live in lowland areas, the Somali of the Ogaden region, and the Danakil and Falasha, who live in several areas of the country.

As in many nations, the ethnic groups of Ethiopia sometimes are in conflict. Regional wars have been fought over land, religion, and the desire to acquire or

Rural Ethiopians often live in circular dwellings, called *tukuls*, that have pointed thatched roofs.

A Danakil woman, who lives in northeastern Ethiopia, hugs her child.

These boys are of the Amhara group, which has traditionally dominated Ethiopian life.

41

maintain political power. In recent years, however, the struggle has shifted its focus to liberation from the political and economic domination of the Amhara- and Tigre-speaking groups. These peoples historically have been the most powerful ethnic communities in the country.

The Refugee Problem

During the civil war of the 1980s, Ethiopian refugees flooded into neighboring nations, including Sudan, Somalia, and Djibouti. When poor weather conditions and fighting prevented many farmers from planting and harvesting their crops, entire communities moved away in order to escape drought and starvation.

Since the fall of the Mengistu regime in 1991, many peasant families have returned

Coptic priests carry an ornate cross during ceremonies that celebrate the Christian feast of Epiphany, called Timkat in Ethiopia.

to their rural homes from Sudan and Somalia. However, Ethiopia still has a large population of refugees, many of them from the war-torn regions of these two neighboring nations. Many refugees as well as returnees have no shelter and very little food. In addition, many members of Ethiopia's rebel armies have been left with a bleak future, as the civilian economy remains too weak to provide employment. The survival of many refugees and soldiers still depends on relief supplies sent from abroad.

Religion

Nearly half of the people of Ethiopia are members of the Ethiopian Orthodox Church, which belongs to the Monophysite (single-nature) branch of Christianity. The Monophysites split from the main body of Christianity in the sixth century A.D. over the question of whether Jesus was human

In a Sudanese refugee camp, an Ethiopian mother mourns the death of her child.

and divine in one nature or in two separate natures. The Ethiopians supported the single-nature theory. For the average Ethiopian Christian, however, such questions seem distant, and it is the local clergy who play the largest role in daily religious life. Several priests are needed to say the ritual mass, and deacons perform secondary functions in the rite.

About 40 percent of Ethiopians are Muslims, who live mostly in the lowland regions. Islam is practiced in its traditional form along the Red Sea coast, which has been influenced by the cultures of the Arabian Peninsula. In the interior, stretching southward toward Kenya and Somalia, religious customs and observance become less formal, mainly because the lifestyle in these areas often makes it difficult to follow Muslim rules. For example, the month-long, daytime fast—including water—in observance of Ramadan may not be possible for a poor farmer who must work in a harsh climate.

Traditional belief in the power of nature and in a natural life force is shared by about 15 percent of Ethiopians. Even those who support another faith, however, may combine elements of these ancient ideas into their own religious faith.

A unique religious minority—the Ethiopian Jews (called Falasha in Amharic)—believes in a mixture of Judaic and traditional African ideas. This sect does not practice the Talmud (Jewish law) and knows no Hebrew (the traditional language of Jewish religious writings). Falasha scriptures are written in Geez. Although they observe the Jewish feast of Passover, Purim—another Jewish festival—is unknown to them.

In 1984 and 1985, about 8,000 Ethiopian Jews were airlifted to the Jewish state of Israel from Sudan, where the Falasha had fled from Ethiopia's famine and wars. Although they no longer face such dire problems, the Falasha of Israel must make a difficult adjustment to a modern society. Most of the Falasha who remain in Ethiopia live in the Gonder region and in Addis Ababa.

Language and Literature

All Ethiopian languages are related to one another. Some tongues are called Semitic, while others are classified as Hamitic. For many linguists (those who study language),

The head of an Ethiopian monastery displays an ancient Bible, written in the Geez language.

Courtesy of Tony Fennerty, M.D., and Bogdan Szajkowski, Ph.D.

43

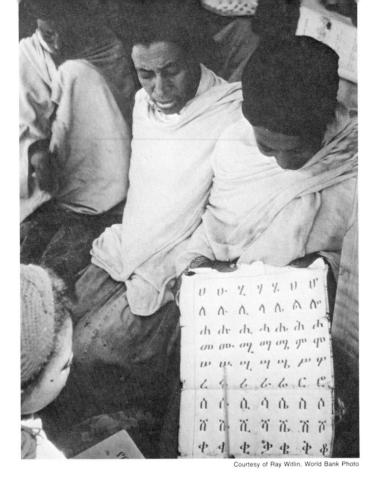

Students are tutored in Amharic, the national tongue of Ethiopia and a member of the Semitic family of languages.

however, these terms simply describe two branches of a single family of languages—the Hamito-Semitic—whose speakers occupy most of northern and eastern Africa and much of the Middle East.

Most of Ethiopia's classical literature is written in Geez and deals mainly with law, philosophy, religion, and history. These writings have been translated from earlier Greek and Arabic texts. Although Geez developed from the original Sabean tongue introduced from Arabia, the ancient Aksumite kingdom used Greek as its official language for a time. Geez did not come into common usage until the Aksumite kingdom was well established.

Health

Like education, health care in Ethiopia is a strong reminder of the need for change. Life expectancy is only about 47 years, and infant mortality is 120 deaths in every

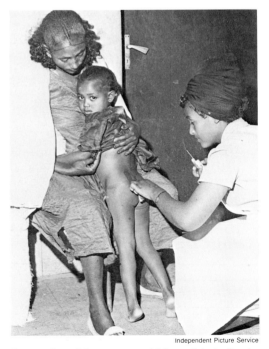

A nurse inoculates a young girl in a clinic in Gonder province.

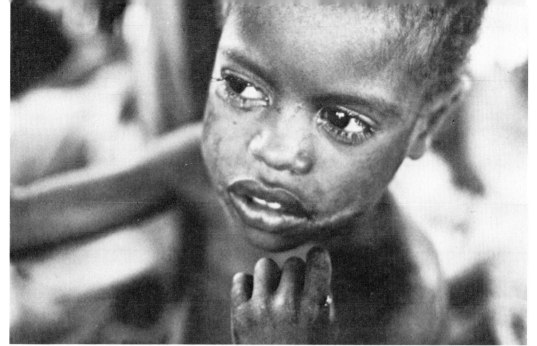

Malnourishment caused by famine has dramatically affected health statistics in northern and southeastern Ethiopia.

1,000 live births. (The average for Africa as a whole is 89 per 1,000.) Ethiopia's health problems will require intense efforts to wipe out diseases such as malaria, tuberculosis, and other ailments related to a lack of basic sanitation facilities. Only 25 percent of the population has access to safe drinking water. Moreover, famine, which still affects parts of rural Ethiopia,

leaves undernourished people especially vulnerable to epidemics.

Government efforts in the area of preventive health care have shown some results since 1975. People in rural areas have been educated about sanitary care, about the preservation of food, and about protecting their wells from contamination. Currently, the government sets aside about

In some rural areas, trained medical personnel travel from village to village to furnish basic health care.

6 percent of the national budget for health care, but much of the money for this service comes from foreign sources.

Education

The slowness of Ethiopia's development is most clear in the area of education. For decades, educational training was offered only to a handful of people, who would later join the royal bureaucracy. With a population of 24 million people in 1970, Ethiopia had enrolled 600,000 children in primary and secondary schools.

In 1975 the governing Derg closed colleges and secondary schools and sent 60,000 students, teachers, and public school officials to the rural areas of Ethiopia. These professionals embarked on the Development Through Cooperation Campaign—known to Ethiopians as the *zemecha* (campaign). The zemecha's goal was to help improve literacy rates and health care, to organize land reform, and to promote the ideas of the newly declared socialist state.

In 1991, when the new government came to power, the zemecha came to an end. The literacy campaign launched in the 1970s, however, has resulted in sharply reduced illiteracy. By the early 1990s, about 70 percent of adult Ethiopians could read and write.

Local peasant associations still control most primary and secondary rural schools. Schooling throughout the country is not yet compulsory. Only about 30 percent of children attend primary school, which begins at age seven and lasts for six years. The percentage of children attending school is even less on the secondary level, which Ethiopian students complete after six years of study. Ethiopia has 11 institutions of higher learning. There are three universities, the largest being the University of Addis Ababa.

Courtesy of American Lutheran Church

In the 1970s, the Derg provided more teachers and launched a nationwide literacy campaign. Here, young children line up to enter their school.

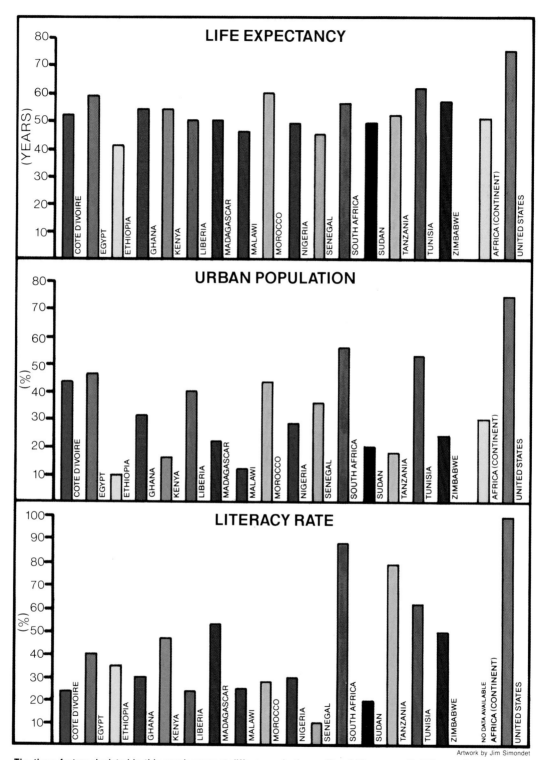

Artwork by Jim Simondet

The three factors depicted in this graph suggest differences in the quality of life among 16 African nations. Averages for the United States and the entire continent of Africa are included for comparison. Data taken from "1987 World Population Data Sheet" and *PC-Globe*.

Grains, particularly maize (corn) and teff, form the basis of the Ethiopian diet.

Courtesy of Agency for International Development

Courtesy of Jeannine Bayard

Batter is poured on a hot griddle to make *injera*, the unleavened bread that is eaten with *wat*, a popular national dish.

Food and Clothing

The staple foods of the country are maize (corn), barley, wheat, and teff (a grain native to Ethiopia). A typical dish in Ethiopian cuisine is *wat*, which is prepared with meat, chicken, and a hot pepper sauce and which is eaten with a kind of bread called *injera*. At high altitudes, lamb is eaten, while goat and camel meat are popular at lower elevations.

Fish, such as Nile perch or tilapia, is caught along the coast and is eaten either cooked or dried. Although wheat is grown, flour is commonly produced from teff, which is made into unleavened bread, such as injera, or into noodles. Popular beverages include coffee, tea, *tej* (a spiced wine), and barley-based beer, called *tella*.

Many Ethiopians in urban areas dress in the Western way, but for important occasions or for a national ceremony, they may wear the *shamma*, a one-piece, cotton gown with a brightly colored border. People in rural areas generally wear the traditional robes of their region, which sometimes are decorated with beads or shells.

Courtesy of American Lutheran Church

Wearing a shamma—a long cotton gown draped around the body like a Roman toga—an Ethiopian reads to a group of listeners.

Courtesy of American Lutheran Church

With the Ethiopian countryside in the background, an elderly musician performs on a *masenko*, which has only one string and is played with a bow.

The Arts

In a country where many people are unable to read, the acting out of religious and historical events has been especially important. The first Western-style drama—a comedy based on the fables of the French writer Jean de La Fontaine—was performed for Emperor Menelik II in Amharic. In the past few decades, names like Debebe Eshetu, Wogayehu Negatu, and Mulatu Astatke have dominated the Ethiopian dramatic scene.

Beautiful Ethiopian songs, written about the land and its people, are accompanied by a variety of instruments, such as the *kerar* (a harplike instrument) and the *masenko* (akin to a violin). The latter has only one string and is played with a bow. The *meleket*, a type of horn, is the most popular wind instrument and is made of wood covered with animal hide. About

3.5 feet in length, it resembles a combination of an ancient Greek trumpet and a Latin tuba. Much of Ethiopia's music is related to church traditions. In Ethiopian churches the only instruments used are sistrums (metal rattles) and drums to accompany choirs.

Ethiopia has a long tradition of religious and historical painting. Many beautifully illustrated manuscripts remain from the Middle Ages, and the walls of churches and public buildings are adorned with paintings. These artworks show a strong resemblance to Byzantine and Romanesque styles of painting and mosaics. Modern painting is represented by the works of Afewerk Tekle, who is considered one of the most talented artists in Ethiopia. His stained-glass windows in Africa Hall are alive with color.

Courtesy of Tony Fennerty, M.D., and Bogdan Szajkowski, Ph.D.

Many of Ethiopia's religious artworks have a Romanesque style, which features ornamented images that are heavily symbolic.

Courtesy of Ethiopian Tourism Commission

Among Ethiopia's modern artworks are Afewerk Tekle's stained-glass windows in Africa Hall.

A painting of a medieval saint hangs in the church of Debre Berhan Selassie in Gonder.

Most Ethiopians, especially women, are skilled at making household objects such as the *messob,* a decorated stand from which Ethiopian dishes are customarily served. Girls and women commonly weave carpets, and beautiful earthenware pots are also made by hand. Many Ethiopian men are skilled goldsmiths, several of whom are famous for their gold and silver objects used in church services.

Architectural details at Lalibela reveal the sturdy, rock-hewn design of the Ethiopian Orthodox churches in the former capital.

Vendors sell handmade earthenware jars at outdoor markets throughout Ethiopia.

Where foodstuffs and commodities are available, people gather at huge markets to exchange goods, such as spices, jugs, and vegetables.

4) The Economy

After the military coup in 1974, the Ethiopian economic system entered a new phase. The Mengistu government discouraged private ownership of property and encouraged greater control of the economy by the government. Farmland was seized from landlords and distributed to landless farmers. Large- and small-scale industries came under government ownership, and import and export trading—as well as all financial institutions—were also under government control.

The EPRDF coalition that replaced Mengistu's regime in 1991 returned many businesses to private ownership. But the government still controls industries such as mining and petroleum refining. The government also prohibits foreign control of power production, telecommunications, and some service industries such as banking.

To bring inflation under control, the new government cut spending and devalued the Ethiopian currency, the *birr*. The government also lifted all price controls. These actions, along with an increase in exports, have helped the Ethiopian economy to grow as fast as 12 percent a year in the late 1990s.

Agriculture

Farming is the major occupation of about four-fifths of all Ethiopians, though only about 12 percent of the country's land is under cultivation. Much of the food grown in Ethiopia is for family needs and is not sold commercially. Modern equipment is not readily available to small-scale farmers, who use horses, oxen, and basic agricultural tools for plowing and harvesting.

The civil wars of the 1970s and 1980s were a disaster for Ethiopian farmers. The conflict, and a severe drought, devastated the country's fertile land and disrupted the distribution of harvested crops. Lacking transportation to market, many growers were forced to allow their crops to rot. As a result, millions of Ethiopians suffered food shortages and starvation.

Although farmland is state property, Ethiopian peasants may pass the land they farm on to their heirs. In addition, peasants are allowed to sell their food on the open market at prices they set. With more plentiful rainfall and better fertiliz-

A young Ethiopian separates grain from its husks (seed coverings) by allowing the wind to carry away the lighter shells, leaving behind the heavier grain kernels.

ers, Ethiopian farms are producing larger harvests, and the country is moving toward self-sufficiency in food.

Modern machinery is not common among small-scale farmers, who are the majority of Ethiopia's agricultural producers. Here, a tractor clears the way for an irrigation canal.

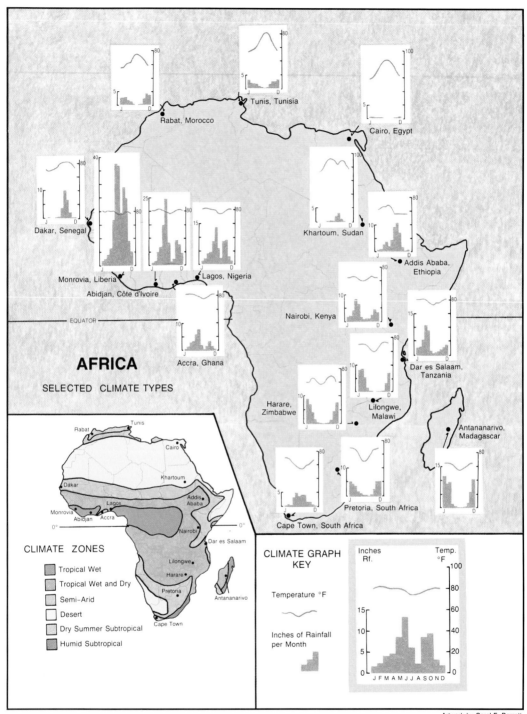

AFRICA

SELECTED CLIMATE TYPES

Rabat, Morocco

Tunis, Tunisia

Cairo, Egypt

Dakar, Senegal

Khartoum, Sudan

Addis Ababa, Ethiopia

Monrovia, Liberia

Abidjan, Côte d'Ivoire

Lagos, Nigeria

Accra, Ghana

EQUATOR

Nairobi, Kenya

Dar es Salaam, Tanzania

Harare, Zimbabwe

Lilongwe, Malawi

Antananarivo, Madagascar

Pretoria, South Africa

Cape Town, South Africa

CLIMATE ZONES

- Tropical Wet
- Tropical Wet and Dry
- Semi-Arid
- Desert
- Dry Summer Subtropical
- Humid Subtropical

Rabat
Tunis
Cairo
Khartoum
Dakar
Addis Ababa
Lagos
Monrovia
Abidjan
Accra
Nairobi
0°
Dar es Salaam
Lilongwe
Harare
Pretoria
Antananarivo
Cape Town

CLIMATE GRAPH KEY

Inches Rf.

Temp. °F

Temperature °F

Inches of Rainfall per Month

J F M A M J J A S O N D

Artwork by Carol F. Barrett

These climate graphs show the monthly change in the average rainfall received and in the average temperature from January to December for the capital cities of 16 African nations. Addis Ababa, Ethiopia, has a tropical wet and dry climate, with the wet season occurring in late summer. The capital is considerably wetter than northern sections of Ethiopia. In addition, Addis Ababa's relatively high altitude moderates its temperatures. Data taken from *World-Climates* by Willy Rudloff, Stuttgart, 1981.

Courtesy of Jeannine Bayard

Most farmers in Ethiopia use oxen and simple tools to plow their fiels.

When water is scarce, the precious liquid is poured directly where it is needed from handmade pitchers.

World Bank Photo

Courtesy of American Lutheran Church

The Derg encouraged the formation of farming cooperatives, which bring more land under cultivation because farmers share the labor of planting and harvesting. The government of Meles Zenawi allowed farmers to vote on disbanding the cooperatives, and by 1998 most farmland was broken up into smaller tracts worked by individual families.

55

Grains, such as teff, wheat, and barley, are grown widely in the highlands from 5,000 to 11,500 feet above sea level. Secondary cereal grains, such as maize, sorghum, and millet, are produced in the western, southwestern, and eastern parts of the country. These regions have the warmer climate and lower altitudes that such crops need. Sorghum and millet also resist drought conditions, growing well in areas that do not receive much rainfall.

Pulses—such as chick-peas, lentils, and haricot beans—grow well at all altitudes but are most often found in the northern and central highlands. Oilseed production has been stimulated by an unlikely source —the Ethiopian Orthodox Church. Its restrictions against the use of animal fats have encouraged the cultivation of vegetable oilseeds, such as linseed, Niger seed, and sesame seed.

Coffee—which originated in Kefa, one of Ethiopia's southern provinces—is a cash crop that accounts for about 40 percent of the nation's export trade. Because of Ethiopia's location within the tropics, citrus fruits, bananas, and vegetables—such as cabbages, onions, peppers, and lettuce— also thrive.

World Bank Photo

Workers stack sheaves of freshly harvested wheat—a staple crop in Ethiopia.

LIVESTOCK

Livestock and animal products—primarily hides and skins—account for 14 percent of Ethiopia's exports, as well as for one-fourth of its agricultural output. In the mid-1990s an estimated 68 million sheep, goats, and cattle grazed on Ethiopia's pastureland, along with about 2.8 million horses and 1 million camels. This livestock total is probably higher than that of any other African country. Drought has decreased these numbers, but by how much is unknown.

Mining and Manufacturing

By the late 1990s, Ethiopia had begun to develop its mineral resources. The Lega

Independent Picture Service

An Ethiopian laborer sorts coffee beans by hand, separating the ripe from the nonripe fruit.

Courtesy of F. Botts, FAO

Large herds of cattle roam Ethiopia's countryside, causing serious soil erosion and deforestation from their constant search for grass-covered pastureland.

Dembi Gold Mine, for example, was the site of preliminary exploration. Mining still accounted for less than 1 percent of the gross domestic product (the total amount of goods produced by a country in a year). The minerals extracted include gold, platinum, salt, limestone, iron, and clay. Adola in southern Ethiopia is famous for its gold mines, and the Danakil Depression in the northeast is renowned for its salt and potash deposits. Ethiopia has underground petroleum reserves, but the

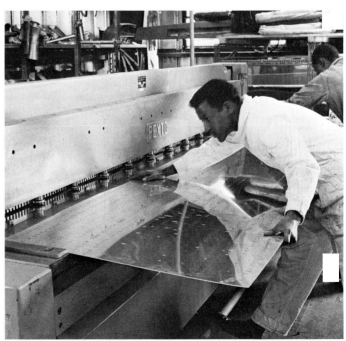

Apprentice sheet-metal workers practice their craft in Addis Ababa, the center of Ethiopia's industrial sector.

Independent Picture Service

Fishermen cast their nets in Lake Awusa, part of the chain of lakes formed by the Great Rift.

government has not yet invested in exploration or drilling.

Food, textiles, and beverages are the main items made in the country. Vegetables, fruit, livestock, and coffee are major export commodities. This area of production is followed by textiles, which are sold mostly within Ethiopia. Other manufactured products include beverages, tobacco, leather shoes, printing, and items made of wood, steel, and cement.

Tourism

For a long time Ethiopia closed its doors to tourists. The country's isolation was most complete during the late 1970s, when internal strife was at its height. In recent years, however, the Ethiopian Tourist Commission has opened up opportunities for foreign visitors to explore the many historical, cultural, and natural phenomena

Surrounded by the raw material of his trade, a merchant breaks up blocks of salt in a marketplace.

Travelers to Ethiopia often visit Gonder, where the baths of Fasilides —the seventeenth-century emperor who founded the city—are a favorite sight.

within present-day Ethiopia. Accompanied by official guides of the commission, foreigners can travel to the castles of Gonder, or visit the churches in Lalibela, or enjoy beautiful views of Blue Nile Gorge and Blue Nile Falls.

Ethiopia has set aside several areas as parkland. The Bale Mountains National Park, in southeastern Ethiopia, includes moorlands, high peaks, alpine lakes, and lava flows. The park is the largest alpine area under protection in Africa.

The waters of Blue Nile Falls plunge over a chasm on their long journey to join the White Nile at Khartoum, Sudan.

Donkeys carry wood – Ethiopia's most common form of household fuel – along a paved road.

The Koka Dam provides hydroelectric power to metropolitan Addis
Ababa.

Energy

Wood and charcoal are the most common fuels for the average Ethiopian. On a large scale, however, the most extensive source of energy is hydroelectric power, which is estimated to provide about 1.2 billion kilowatt-hours a year and has the potential to meet all of Ethiopia's energy needs. The country's location within the tropics also provides the nation with the potential for solar energy.

The country's first hydropower plants were built on the Awash River between 1960 and 1970. In 1974 Ethiopia's largest complex was put into operation on a tributary of the Blue Nile. In the late 1970s the European Economic Community and the United Nations fostered the development of vast geothermal energy sources — located beneath the Great Rift Valley — that use the heat of the earth's interior to provide energy.

Although Ethiopia has few paved roads, a modern highway crosses the Blue Nile and meanders through the rugged landscape.

Transportation

Because of Ethiopia's rugged terrain and seasonal weather problems, highways are few and fail to meet the economic and social needs of the people. Most villages, mineral-rich regions, and agricultural lands are inaccessible. Pack animals, and occasionally airplanes, provide transportation to these isolated regions. Many Ethiopians consider the poor road network one of the nation's major obstacles to development.

Ethiopia's only railroad line—between Addis Ababa and neighboring Djibouti— moves import and export commodities. Water transportation is used in some parts of the country, particularly around Lake Tana and the Rift Valley lakes and on rivers in the south. Ethiopian Air Lines handles transportation from Addis Ababa to major cities within Ethiopia and to parts of Africa, Europe, and Asia.

Courtesy of Ethiopian Tourism Commission

Independent Picture Service

The planes of Ethiopian Air Lines (EAL) sometimes are used to transport equipment and supplies to isolated areas.

Rains and flooding affect travel, and occasionally even sturdy jeeps are unable to cross streams to safer ground.

Courtesy of Jeannine Bayard

Courtesy of Tony Fennerty, M.D., and Bogdan Szajkowski, Ph.D.

Tankwas, boats made of papyrus reeds, are the main form of transportation on Lake Tana.

Despite the occasional good harvest, stockpiles of food in Ethiopia have never caught up with continued demand. As a result, famine and loss of life—especially among young children—still threaten Ethiopia's immediate future.

The Future

As one of the few African nations that can trace its history to ancient times, Ethiopia continues to fascinate historians. But the country's more recent history has troubled the world with a very different image. Many Ethiopians have died of hunger or disease. Many others have become refugees in neighboring countries. By the 1990s, however, the country was producing more food and depending less on foreign aid to sustain its population.

The end of a long civil war offers Ethiopia's new leaders an opportunity for economic success. Yet many obstacles remain, including a poor transportation system, a heavy burden of foreign debt, and the loss of ports in independent Eritrea. In addition, rivalries between Ethiopia's ethnic groups remain a serious threat to stability. But with the return of economic growth, Ethiopia has a chance to tap its vast human and natural resources as the twenty-first century begins.

Index